LADY GAGA

CHROMATICA

T0070839

ISBN 978-1-70510-784-3

Visit Hal Leonard Online at
www.halleonard.com

Contact us:
Hal Leonard
7777 West Bluemound Road
Milwaukee, WI 53213
Email: info@halleonard.com

In Europe, contact:
Hal Leonard Europe Limited
42 Wigmore Street
Marylebone, London, W1U 2RN
Email: info@halleonardeurope.com

In Australia, contact:
Hal Leonard Australia Pty. Ltd.
4 Lentara Court
Cheltenham, Victoria, 3192 Australia
Email: info@halleonard.com.au

CONTENTS

CHROMATICA I

Words and Music by STEFANI GERMANOTTA
and MORGAN KIBBY

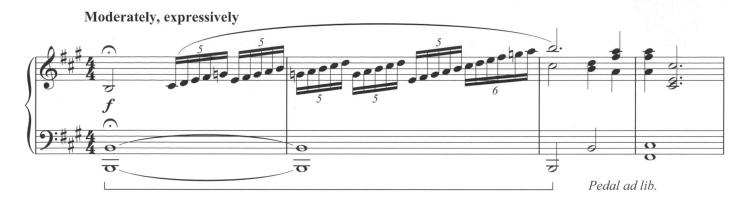

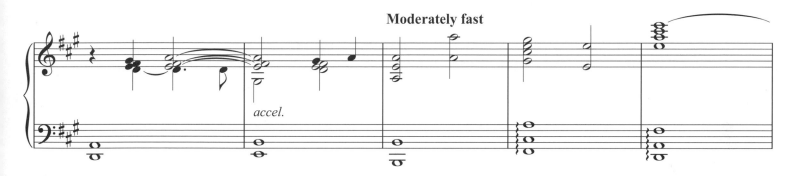

ALICE

Words and Music by STEFANI GERMANOTTA,
MICHAEL TUCKER, AXEL HEDFORS,
JOHANNES KLAHR and JUSTIN TRANTER

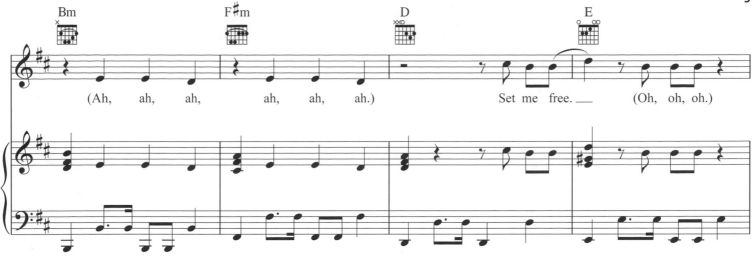

(Ah, ah, ah, ah, ah, ah.) Set me free. ___ (Oh, oh, oh.)

(Ah, ah, ah, ah, ah, ah.) Set me free. ___

___ (Oh, oh, oh.) Could you pull me out ___ of this ___ a - live? ___

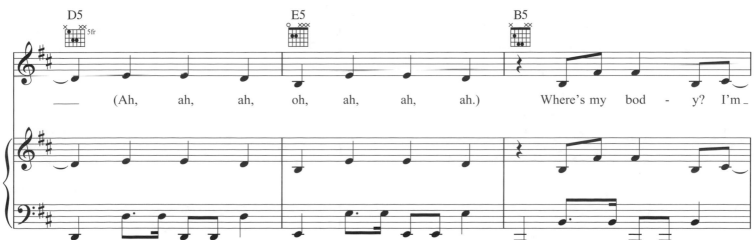

___ (Ah, ah, ah, oh, ah, ah, ah.) Where's my bod - y? I'm ___

stuck in ___ my mind. ___ (Ah, ah, ah, oh, ah, ah, ah.)

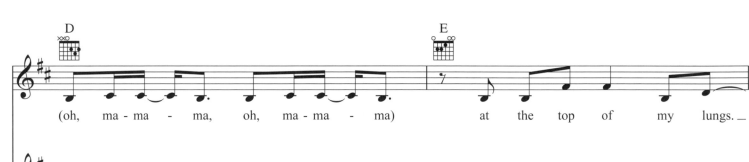

(Oh, ma - ma - ma, oh, ma - ma - ma.) I'm tired of scream - ing

(oh, ma - ma - ma, oh, ma - ma - ma) at the top of my lungs. ___

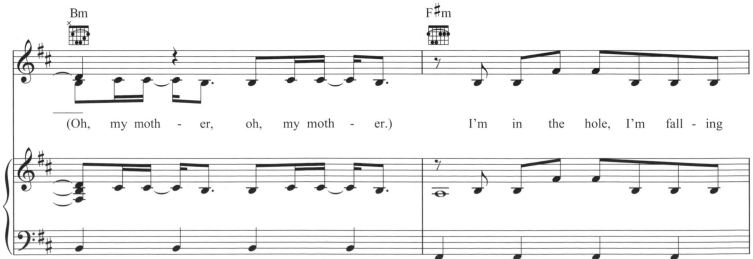

(Oh, my moth - er, oh, my moth - er.) I'm in the hole, I'm fall - ing

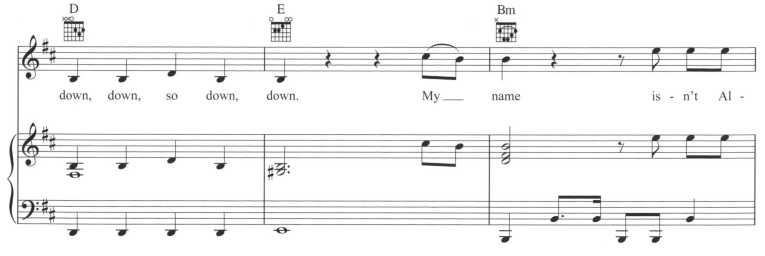

down, down, so down, down. My ___ name is - n't Al -

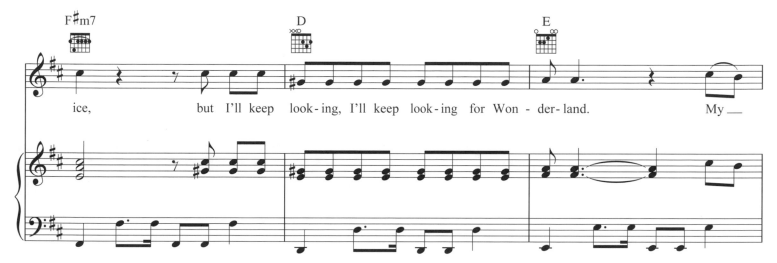

ice, but I'll keep look - ing, I'll keep look - ing for Won - der - land. My ___

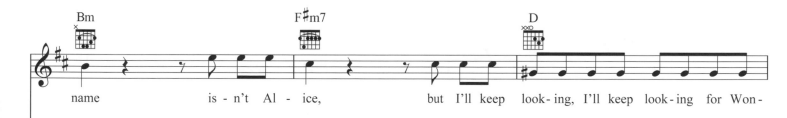

name is - n't Al - ice, but I'll keep look - ing, I'll keep look - ing for Won -

der - land, Won - der - land. Take me ___ home. ___ Take

STUPID LOVE

Words and Music by STEFANI GERMANOTTA,
MAX MARTIN, MICHAEL TUCKER,
MARTIN BRESSO and ELY WEISFIELD

Kinda hard to believe, got to have faith in me.)
I would battle for you, even if I break in two.)

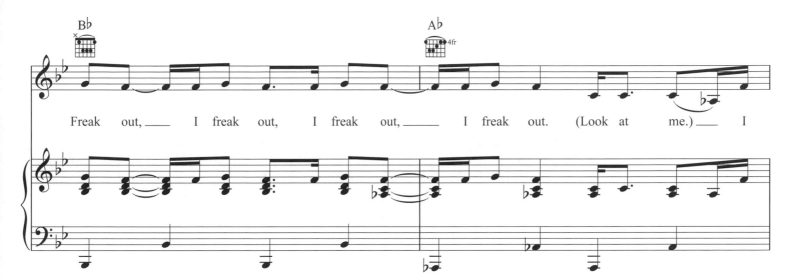

Freak out, I freak out, I freak out, I freak out. (Look at me.) I

get down, I get down, I get down, I get down. (Look at me.) I

freak out, I freak out, I freak out, I freak out. Look at me

now. _____ 'Cause all I ev - er want - ed was love. ____ Ooh. ____
(Hey yah __ yah)

____ Ooh. ____ All I ev - er want - ed was love. _
(Hey yah __ yah) (Hey yah __ yah)

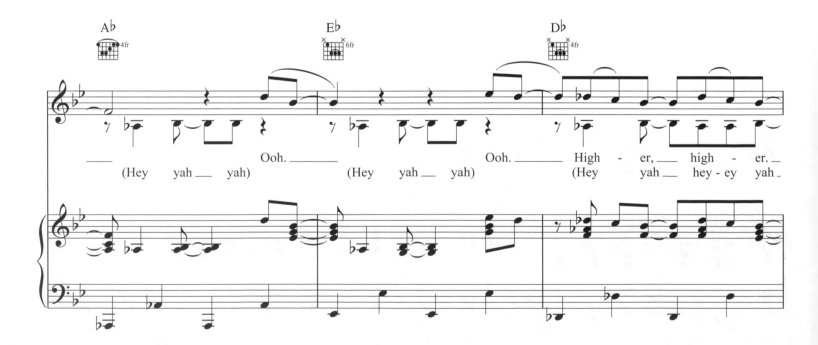

____ Ooh. ____ Ooh. ____ High - er, high - er. _
(Hey yah __ yah) (Hey yah __ yah) (Hey yah __ hey - ey yah _

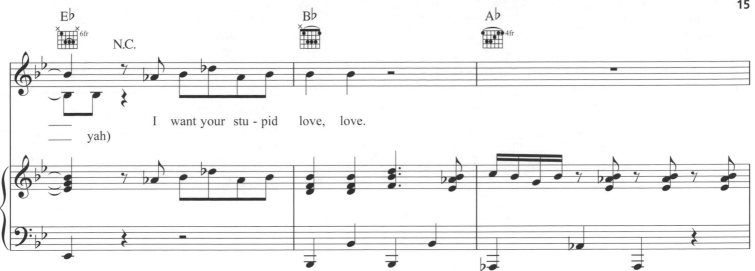

I want your stu-pid love, love.
___ yah)

I want your stu-pid love, love.

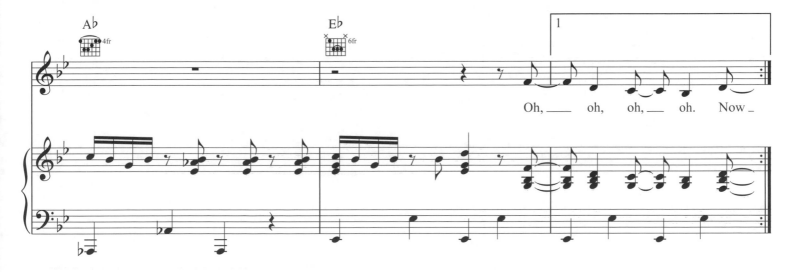

Oh, ___ oh, oh, ___ oh. Now ___

___ oh, oh, ___ oh. I don't need a rea-son. ___

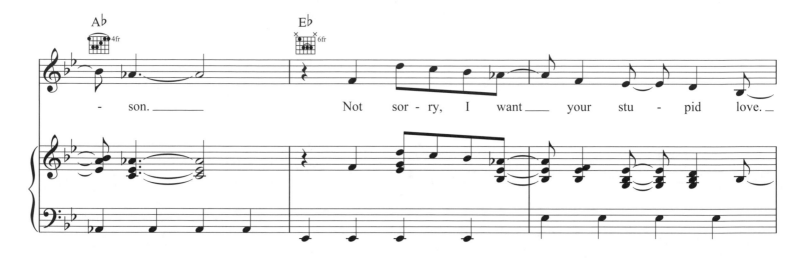

Not sor-ry, I want your stu-pid love. I don't need a rea-

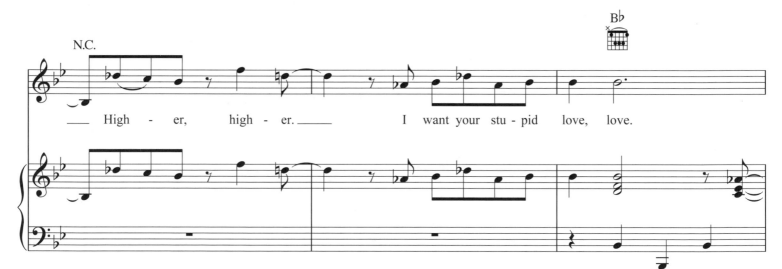

-son. Not sor-ry, I want your stu-pid love.

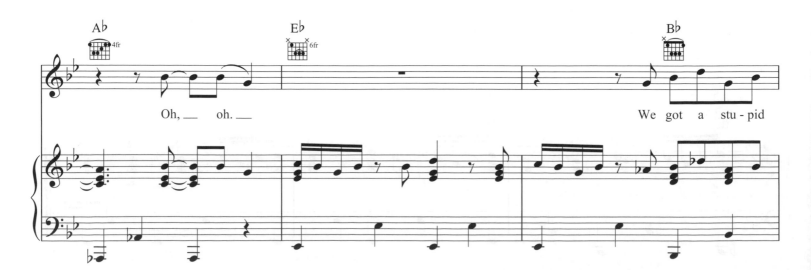

High-er, high-er. I want your stu-pid love, love.

Oh, oh. We got a stu-pid

love, love, love, love, __ oh. __ Oh, _

_ oh, I want your stu-pid love, love. Oh, oh, ___ oh, oh, oh, oh,

oh, oh, oh, oh, ___ oh. I want your stu-pid love, love.

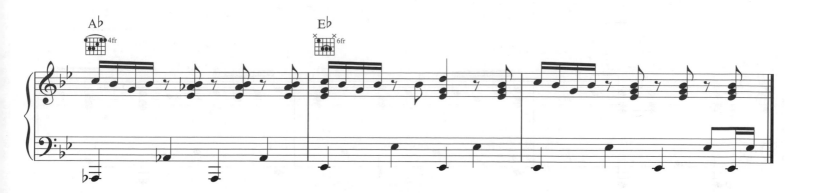

RAIN ON ME

Words and Music by STEFANI GERMANOTTA,
MATTHEW BURNS, MARTIN BRESSO,
MICHAEL TUCKER, RAMI YACOUB,
ARIANA GRANDE and NIJA CHARLES

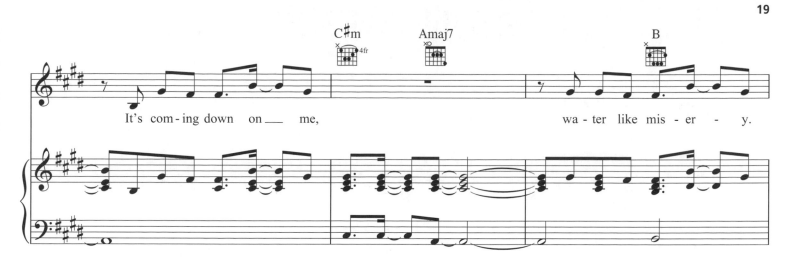

It's com-ing down on ___ me, wa-ter like mis-er-y.

It's com-ing down on ___ me.

I'd rath-er be dry, ___ but at least I'm a-live. ___ Rain

I'm read-y; rain on ___ me.

on me, rain, rain, rain on ___ me, rain, rain. I'd rath-er be dry, ___ but at

least I'm a - live. ___ Rain on me, rain, rain. Rain on

me.

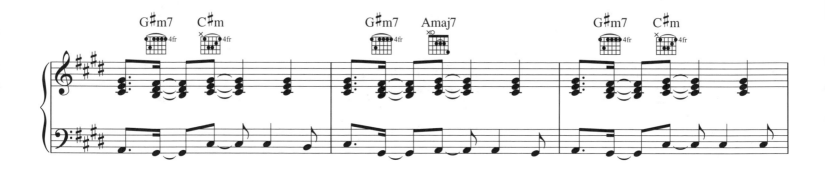

Rain on me. Liv-ing in a world where no one's

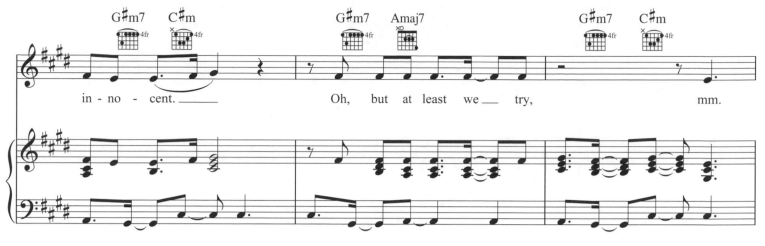

in - no - cent. _____ Oh, but at least we _____ try, _____ mm.

Got - ta live my truth, not keep it bot - tled in _____ so I don't lose my _____ mind,

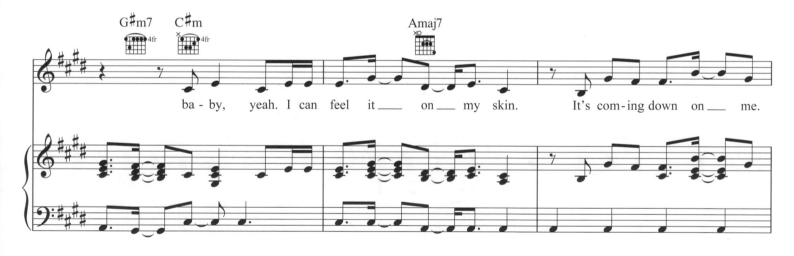

ba - by, yeah. I can feel it _____ on _____ my skin. It's com - ing down on _____ me.

Tear - drops _____ on _____ my face. Wa - ter like mis - er - y. Let it wash a - way _____ my sins. _____

It's com-ing down on ___ me. Let it wash a - way. _____ I'd

Rain on me. Rain on me.

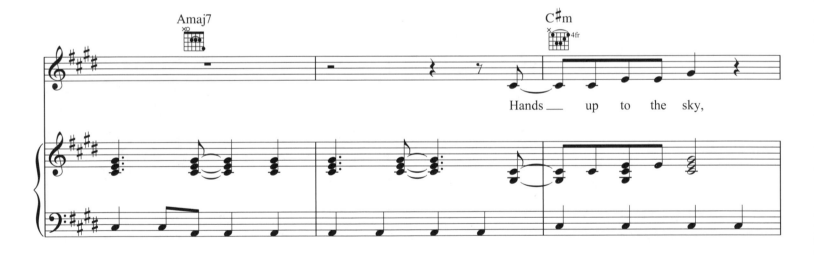

Hands ___ up to the sky,

I'll be your gal - ax - y. I'm ___ a - bout to fly. Rain on me, tsu - na - mi. Hands ___

up to the sky, ___ I'll be your gal-ax-y. I'm ___ a-bout to fly. ___

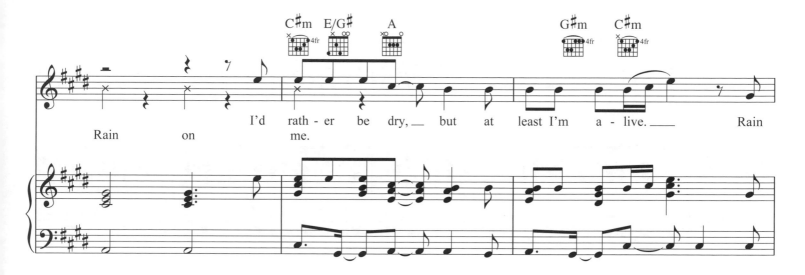

Rain   on   me.   I'd rath-er be dry, ___ but at least I'm a-live. ___ Rain

on me, rain, rain, rain on me, rain, rain. I'd rath-er be dry, ___ but at

least I'm a-live. ___ Rain on me, rain, rain. Rain on

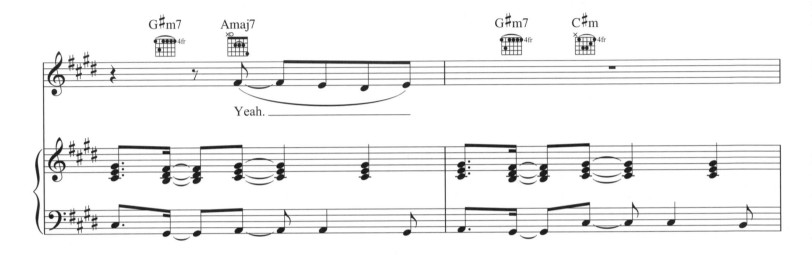

FREE WOMAN

Words and Music by STEFANI GERMANOTTA,
MICHAEL TUCKER, AXEL HEDFORS
and JOHANNES KLAHR

Moderately fast

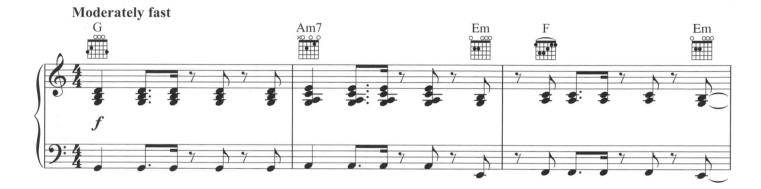

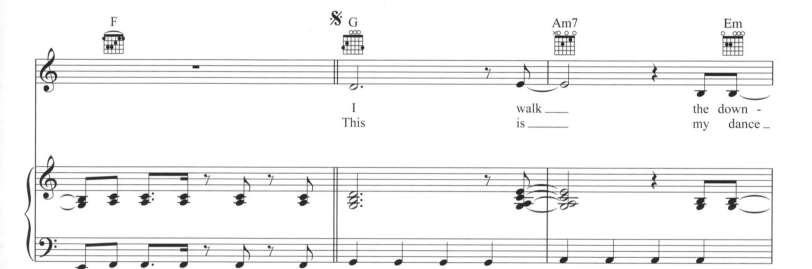

knows me ___ yet,   not right ___ now.   But
that's what ___ I'm   liv - ing ___ for.   So

I am   bound to set ___ this feel - ing   in mo -
light up   my bod - y ___ and kiss ___ me   too hard -

To Coda

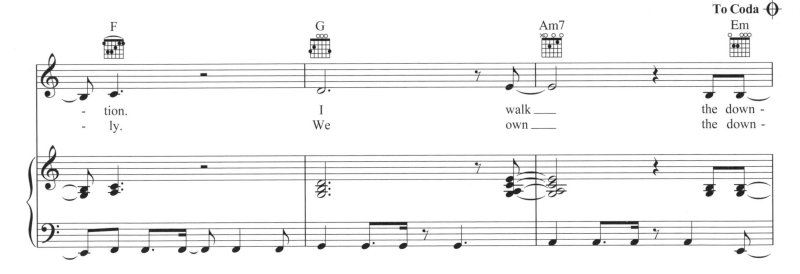

- tion.   I   walk ___ the down -
- ly.   We   own ___ the down -

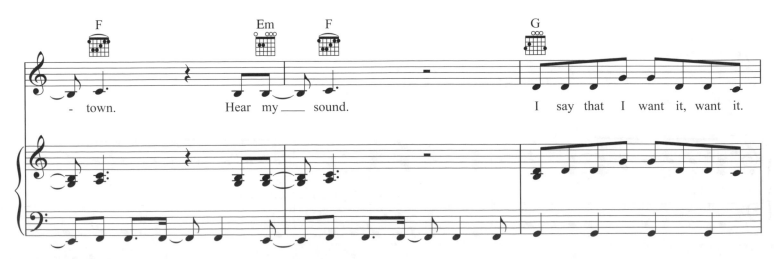

- town.   Hear my ___ sound.   I say that I want it, want it.

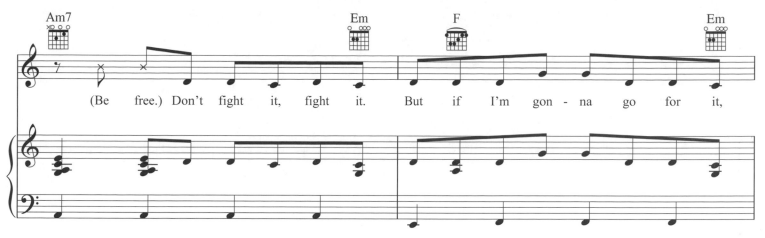

(Be free.) Don't fight it, fight it. But if I'm gon-na go for it,

I'll re-mem-ber that, that,... I say that I want it, want it. (Be free.) Don't fight it, fight it.

But if I'm gon-na go for it, I'll re-mem-ber that, that I, I'm not noth-ing with -

out a stead-y hand. I'm not noth-ing un-less I know_ I can.

I'm still some-thing if I don't got ___ a man. I'm a free wom - an. ___ Uh, ooh. ___

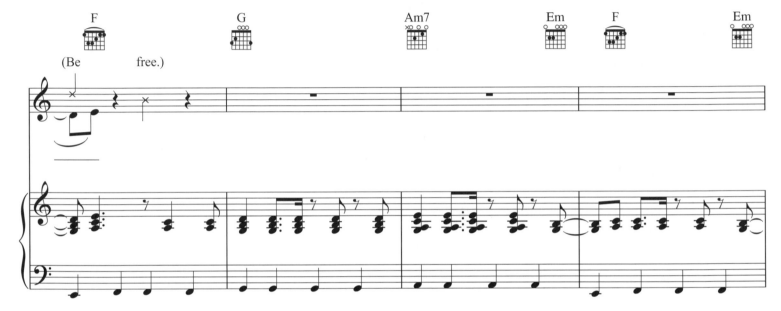

(Be free.)

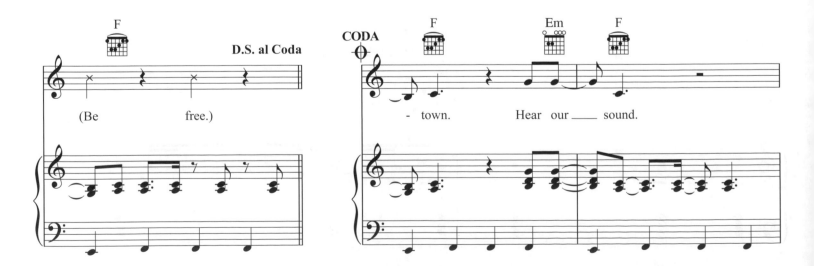

(Be free.) D.S. al Coda

CODA

- town. Hear our ___ sound.

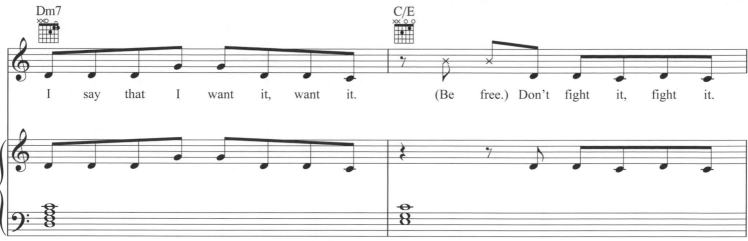

I say that I want it, want it. (Be free.) Don't fight it, fight it.

But if I'm gon-na go for it, I'll re-mem-ber that, that,... I say that I want it, want it.

(Be free.) Don't fight it, fight it. But if I'm gon-na go for it, I'll re-mem-ber that, that I,

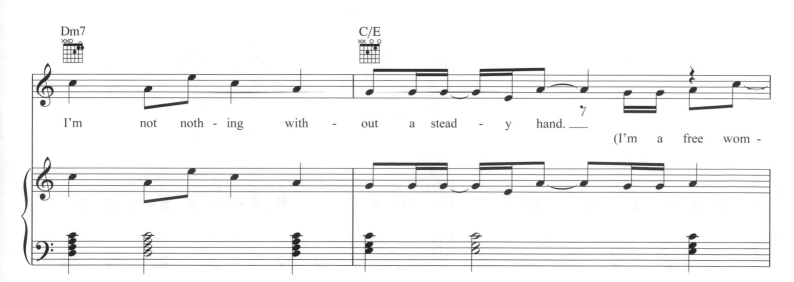

I'm not noth-ing with-out a stead-y hand. ___ (I'm a free wom-

I'm   not noth - ing un - less I know I can. _____
- an.)   (I'm a free wom -

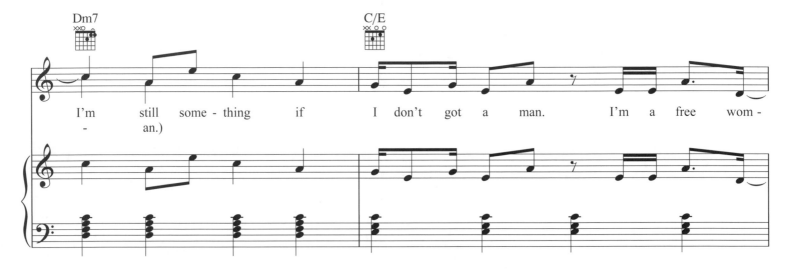

I'm   still some - thing if   I don't got a man.   I'm a free wom -
- an.)

- an. _____   Uh, ooh. _____   Come on! I'm a free wom - an. _____
                  (Be   free.)

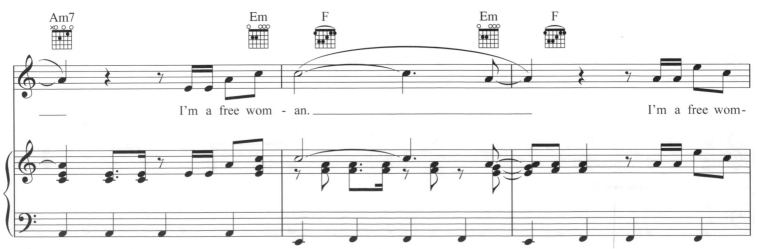

_____ I'm a free wom - an. _____   I'm a free wom-

a-, ee - a - ee - a - ee - a - ee - a - a-, an. _____ I'm a free wom -

- an. _____ Uh, ooh. _____ Oh, yeah, I'm a free wom -

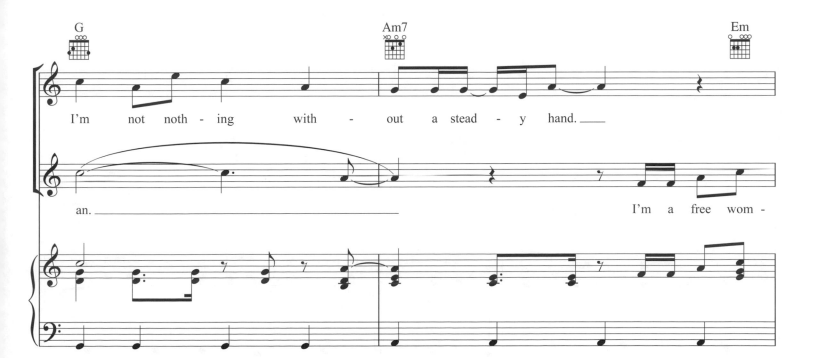

I'm not noth-ing with-out a stead-y hand. ____

an. _____ I'm a free wom -

FUN TONIGHT

Words and Music by STEFANI GERMANOTTA,
MATTHEW BURNS, MICHAEL TUCKER
and RAMI YACOUB

Recorded a half step lower.

I can't ___ see straight, ___ I can't ___ see me. ___ There's too ___ much hurt ___

___ caught in ___ be - tween. ___ Wish I ___ could be ___

___ what I know ___ I am. ___ This mo - ment's hi - jacked my ___ plans.

I'm feel - ing the way that I'm feel - ing, I'm feel - ing with

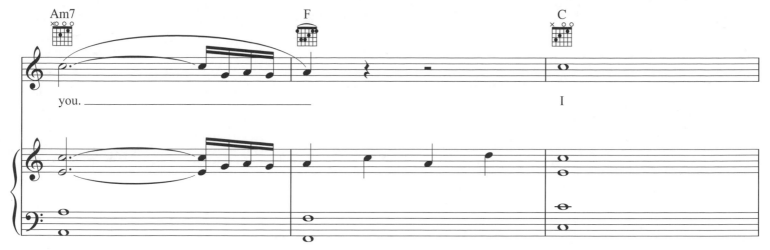

you. _____ I

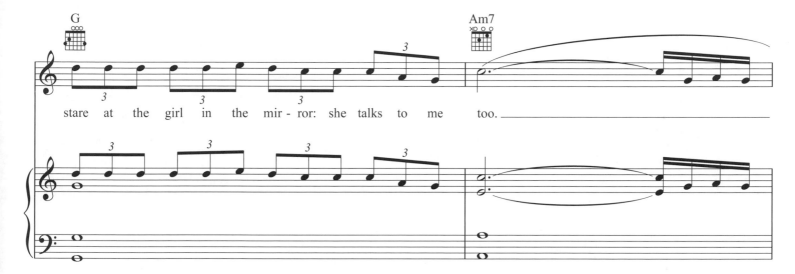

stare at the girl in the mir - ror: she talks to me too. _____

_____ Yeah, I can see it in your face. You don't think I pull my weight.

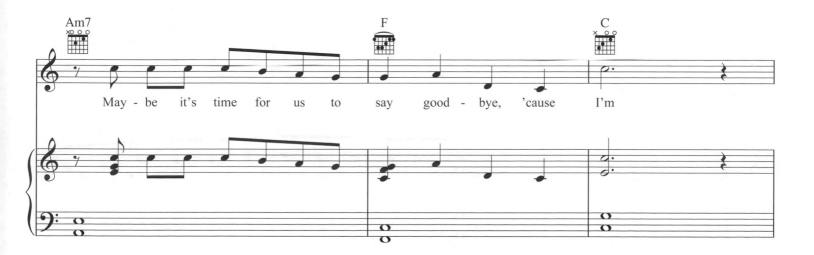

May - be it's time for us to say good - bye, 'cause I'm

feel-ing the way that I'm feel-ing, I'm feel-ing with you._____

To Coda ⊕
N.C.
_____ I'm not hav-ing fun to-night._____ You love the pa-pa-raz-zi,

love the fame,_____ e-ven though you know it caus-

es me pain._____ I feel like I'm in a

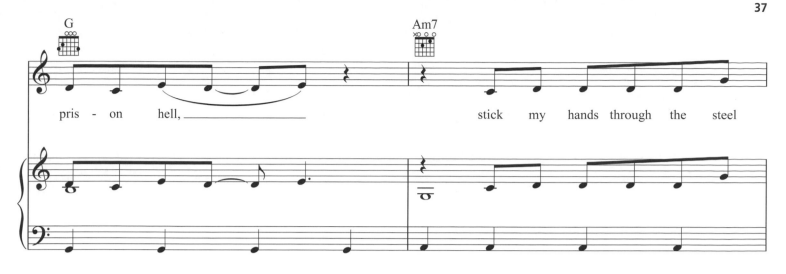

pris - on hell, _____ stick my hands through the steel

bars and yell. What hap - pens now?_ I'm not_ o - kay._

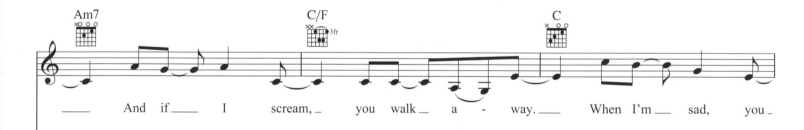

_ And if_ I scream,_ you walk_ a - way._ When I'm_ sad, you_

D.S. al Coda

_ just wan - na play._ I've had_ e - nough._ Why do_ I stay?

CHROMATICA II

Words and Music by STEFANI GERMANOTTA
and MORGAN KIBBY

Moderately, expressively

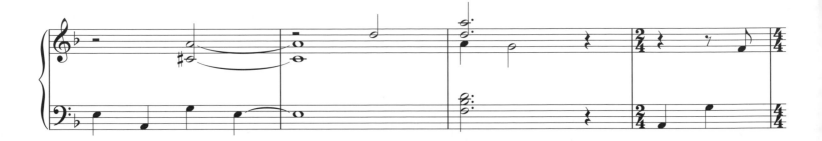

Quickly

911

Words and Music by STEFANI GERMANOTTA,
MICHAEL TUCKER, JUSTIN TRANTER
and HUGO LECLERCQ

* *Lead vocal sung an octave lower.*

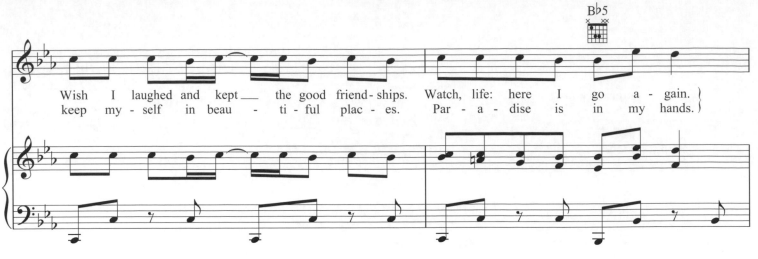

Wish I laughed and kept the good friend-ships. Watch, life: here I go a-gain.
keep my-self in beau-ti-ful plac-es. Par-a-dise is in my hands.

I can't see me cry, can't see me cry ev-er a-gain

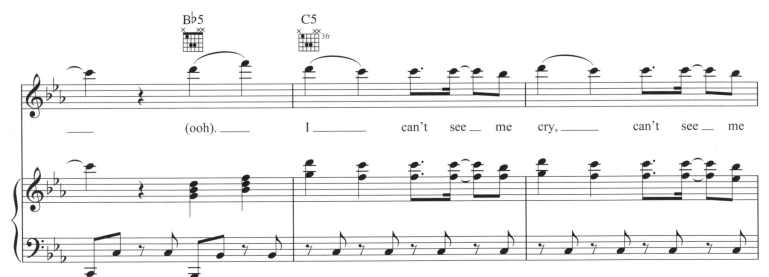

(ooh). I can't see me cry, can't see me

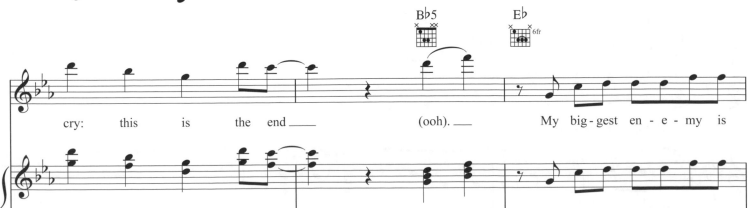

cry: this is the end (ooh). My big-gest en-e-my is

cry, ___ can't see ___ me cry ev - er a - gain ___ (ooh). ___

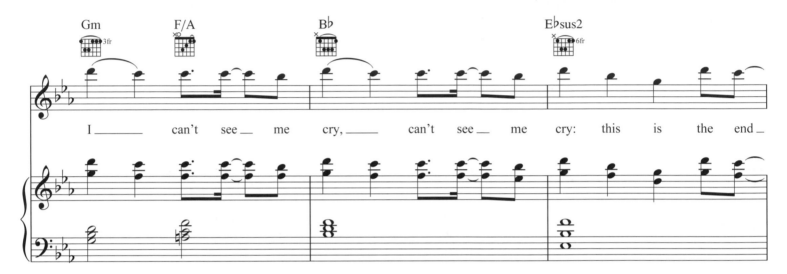

I ___ can't see ___ me cry, ___ can't see ___ me cry: this is the end ___

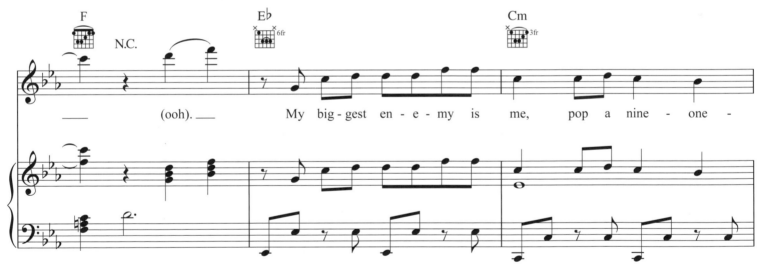

___ (ooh). ___ My big - gest en - e - my is me, pop a nine - one -

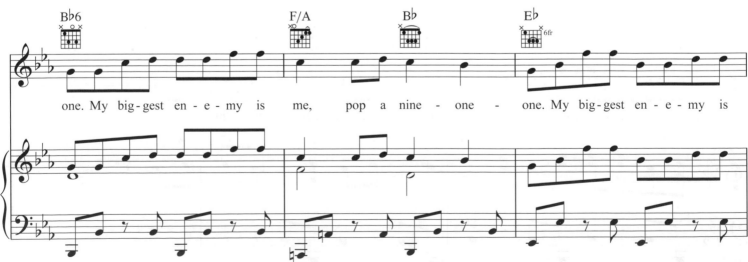

one. My big - gest en - e - my is me, pop a nine - one - one. My big - gest en - e - my is

me, ev - er since day one. Pop a nine - one - one, then pop an - oth - er one.

Please, patch the line, _____ please, patch the line. _____ Need a nine - one -

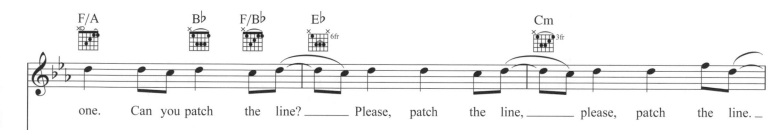

one. Can you patch the line? _____ Please, patch the line, _____ please, patch the line. _

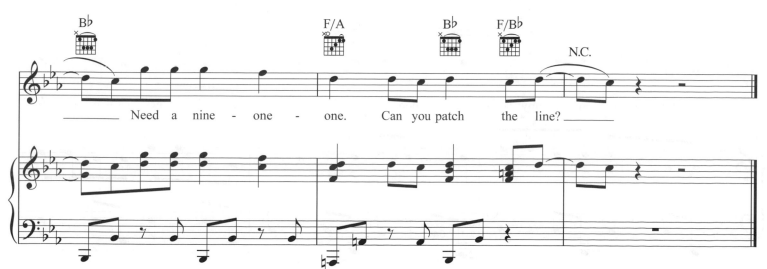

_____ Need a nine - one - one. Can you patch the line? _____

PLASTIC DOLL

Words and Music by STEFANI GERMANOTTA,
MICHAEL TUCKER, SONNY JOHN MOORE,
RAMI YACOUB and JACOB HINDLIN

too long danc - ing all a - lone, danc - ing to the same song.

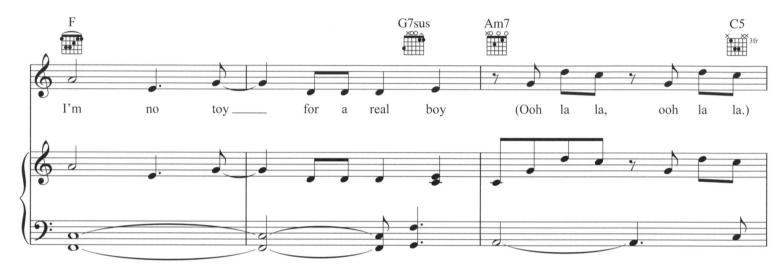

I'm no toy ____ for a real boy (Ooh la la, ooh la la.)

If you're a real __ boy, don't play with me; _____ it just

hurts me. _____ I'm bounc-ing off the walls. __ No, no, no,

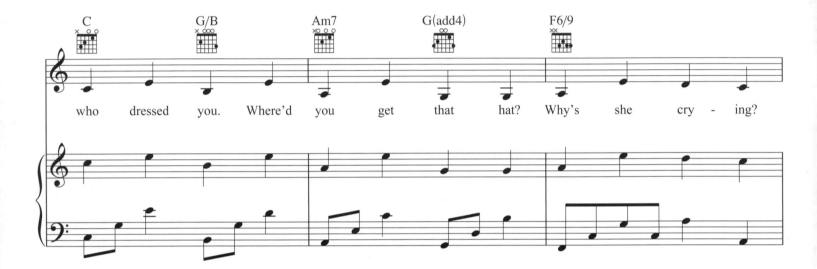

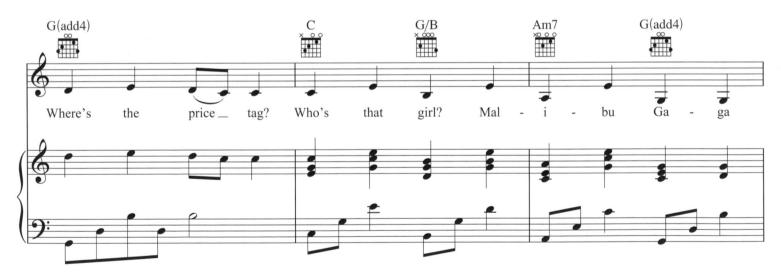

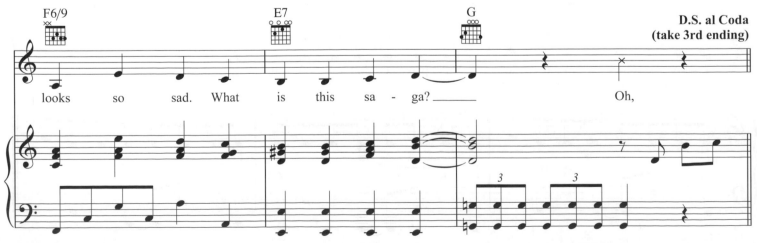

(Am I - ee, I - ee, I - ee, I - ee, I, am I p-, plas - tic?

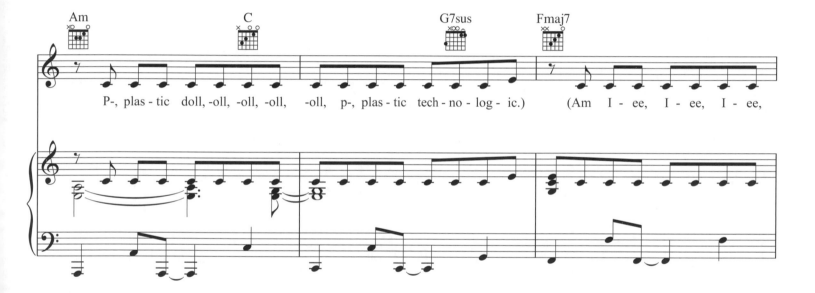

P-, plas - tic doll, -oll, -oll, -oll, -oll, p-, plas - tic tech - no - log - ic.) (Am I - ee, I - ee, I - ee,

I - ee, I, am I p-, plas - tic? P-, plas - tic doll, -oll, -oll, -oll, -oll, p-, plas - tic tech - no - log - ic.)

SOUR CANDY

Words and Music by STEFANI GERMANOTTA,
MATTHEW BURNS, HONG JUN PARK,
MICHAEL TUCKER, RAMI YACOUB
and MADISON LOVE

nal po - jan - ghan geon __ neo - ya, neo - ya.
so - ri - jil - leo - wa, __ uh - huh, uh - huh.

Oh, _____ I'm hard on the out - side, but if you give me __

__ time, then I could make __ time for __ your love. __ I'm hard on the out -

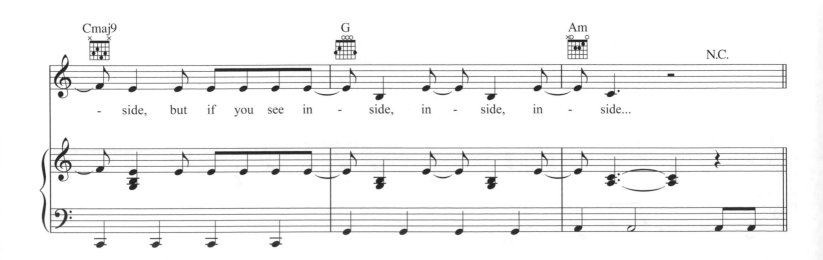

- side, but if you see in - side, in - side, in - side...

time, then I could make __ time for __ your love. __ I'm hard on the out-

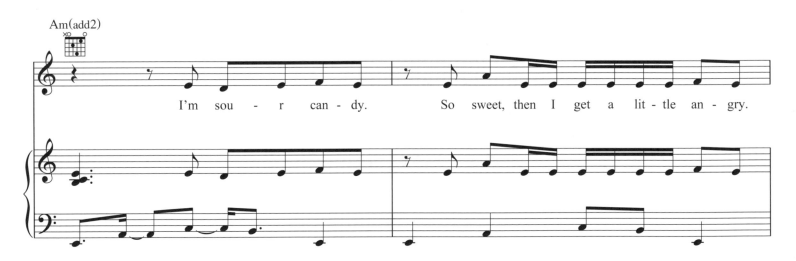

- side, but if you see in - side, in - side, in - side...

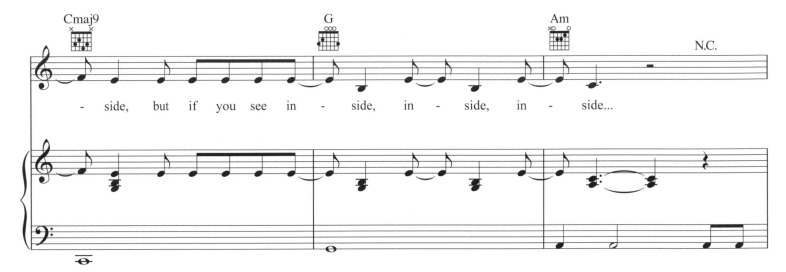

I'm sou - r can - dy. So sweet, then I get a lit - tle an - gry.

Yeah, sou - r can - dy. Yeah, yeah, __ yeah, __ yeah, yeah. I'm su - per psy - cho,

ENIGMA

Words and Music by STEFANI GERMANOTTA,
MATTHEW BURNS, JACOB HINDLIN
and MICHAEL TUCKER

O - pen mind - ed. I'm so blind - ed. Mys - ter - y man,
Can't stop star - ing, I'm so na - ked. Wrapped in shad - ows,

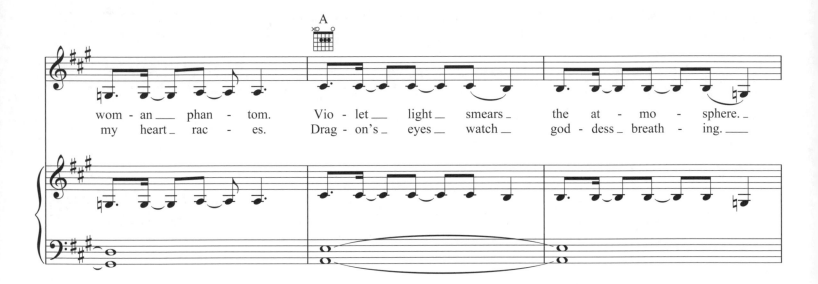

wom - an phan - tom. Vio - let light smears the at - mo - sphere.
my heart rac - es. Drag - on's eyes watch god - dess breath - ing.

I'm so scared, but I'm stand - ing here.
Give me some - thing to be - lieve in.

Is what I'm see - ing real,

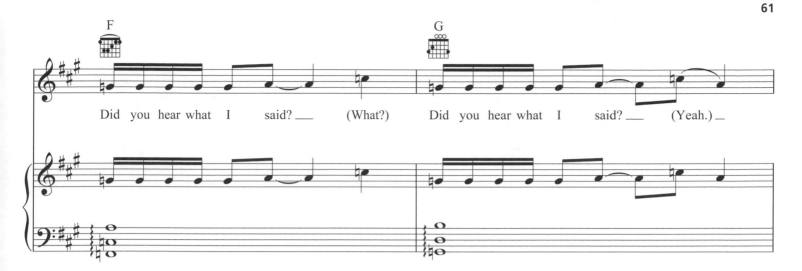

Did you hear what I said? __ (What?) Did you hear what I said? __ (Yeah.) __

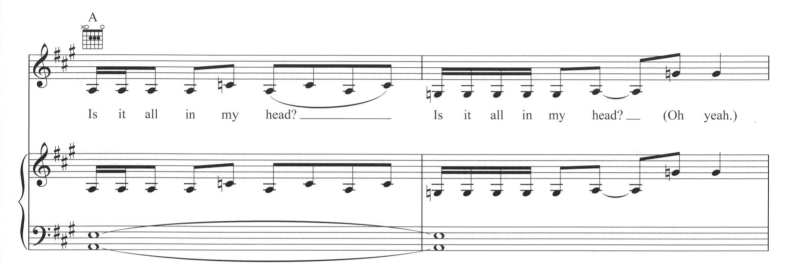

Is it all in my head? _____ Is it all in my head? __ (Oh yeah.)

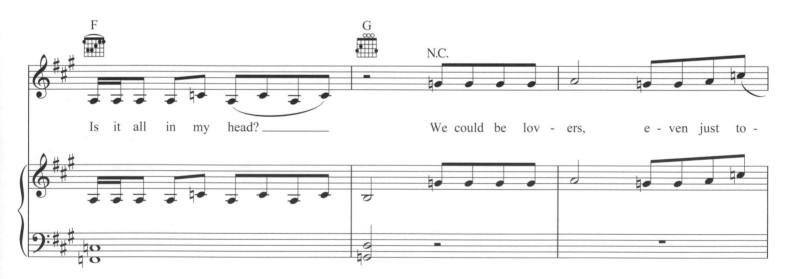

Is it all in my head? _____ We could be lov - ers, e - ven just to -

- night. We could be an - y - thing __ you __ want. __ We could be jok -

REPLAY

Words and Music by STEFANI GERMANOTTA,
MATTHEW BURNS and MICHAEL TUCKER

Moderately fast

Am I still a-live? "Where am I?", I cry. Who was it that pulled the trig-ger? Was it you or I? I'm com-plete-ly numb. Why you act-ing dumb? I won't blame my-self, 'cause we __ both know that you're the one.

* *Recorded a half step lower.*

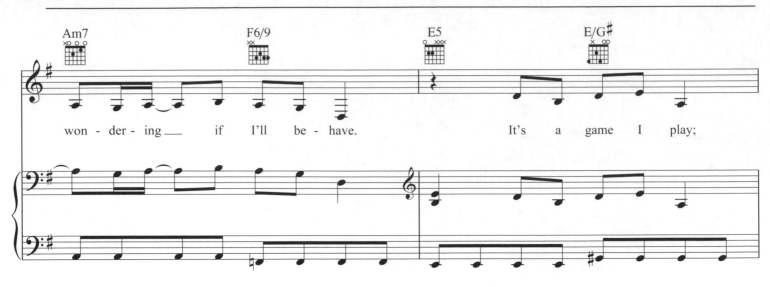

won-der-ing___ if I'll be-have.   It's a game I play;

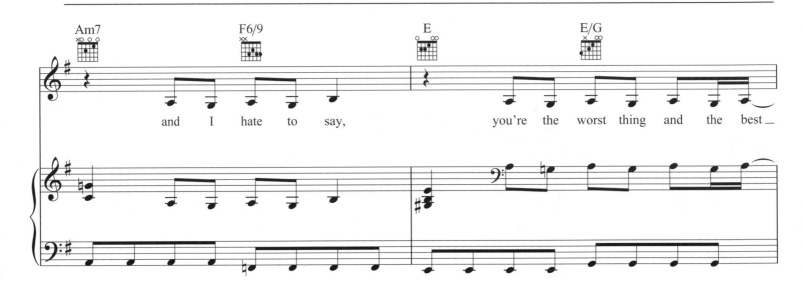

and I hate to say,   you're the worst thing and the best___

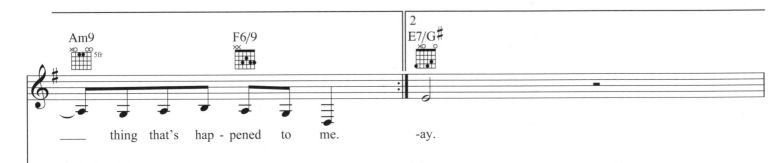

___ thing that's hap-pened to me.   -ay.

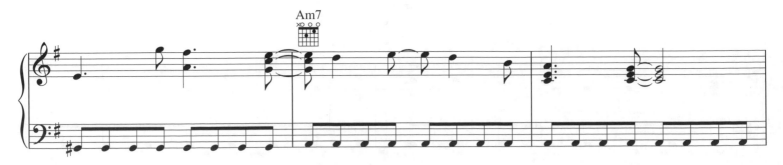

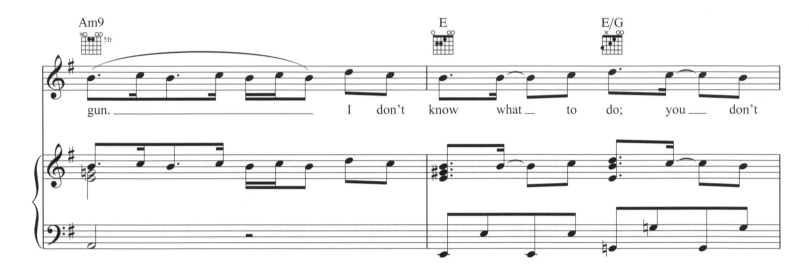

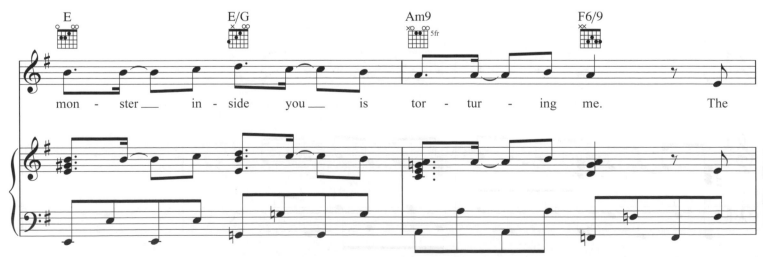

scars on ___ my mind are ___ on re - play, ___ re-, re - play, ___ -ay,

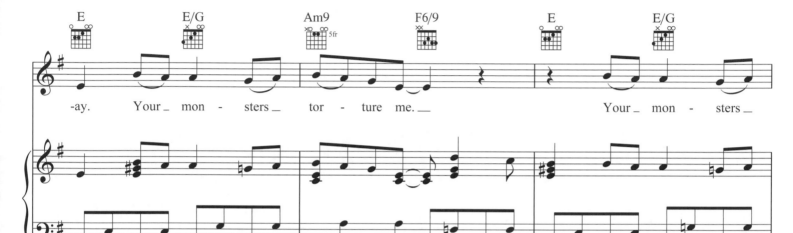

-ay. Your ___ mon - sters ___ tor - ture me. ___ Your ___ mon - sters ___

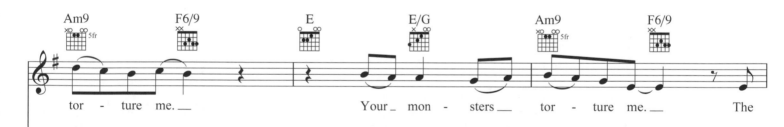

tor - ture me. ___ Your ___ mon - sters ___ tor - ture me. ___ The

scars on ___ my mind are ___ on re - play, ___ re-, re - play. ___

CHROMATICA III

Words and Music by STEFANI GERMANOTTA
and MORGAN KIBBY

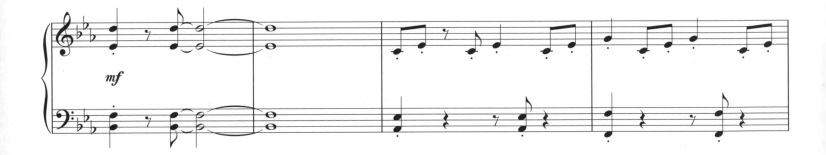

SINE FROM ABOVE

Words and Music by STEFANI GERMANOTTA,
BENJAMIN RICE, ELTON JOHN,
SALEM AL FAKIR, AXEL HEDFORS,
SEBASTIAN INGROSSO, JOHANNES KLAHR,
RICHARD ZASTENKER, VINCENT PONTE,
RYAN TEDDER, MICHAEL TUCKER
and RAMI YACOUB

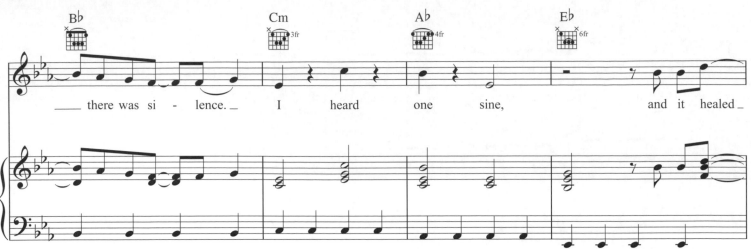

there was si - lence. __ I heard one sine, and it healed __

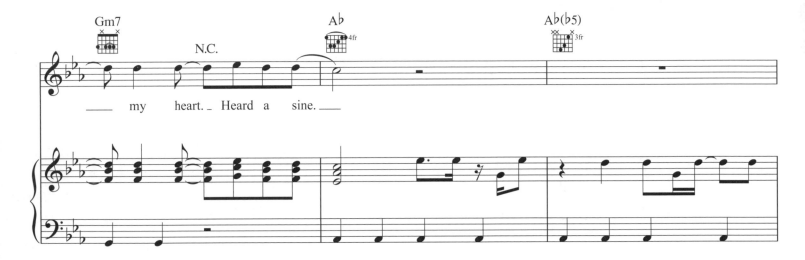

__ my heart. __ Heard a sine. __

Healed __ my heart. __ Heard a sine. ___

To Coda

Healed __ my heart, __ heard a sine. __

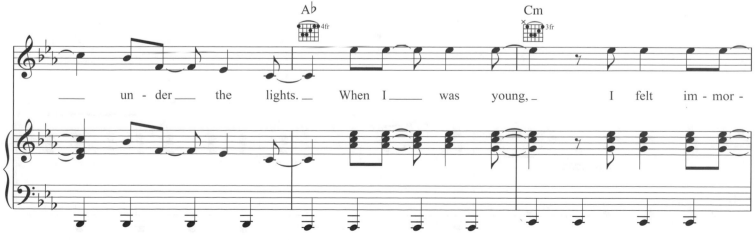

1000 DOVES

Words and Music by STEFANI GERMANOTTA,
MARTIN BRESSO, MICHAEL TUCKER
and RAMI YACOUB

Moderately fast

I need you to lis-ten to___ me. Please___ be-lieve___ me, I'm com-

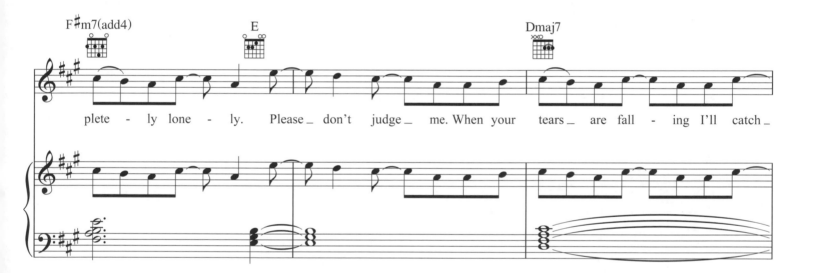

plete-ly lone-ly. Please___ don't judge___ me. When your tears___ are fall-ing I'll catch___

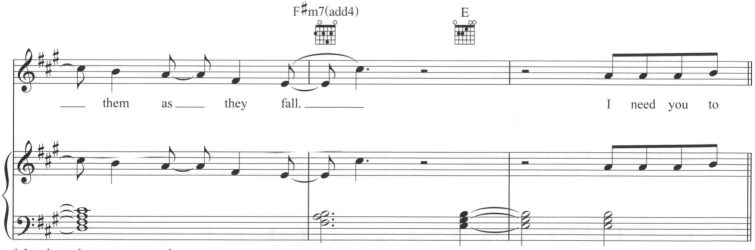

___ them as___ they fall.___ I need you to

Lead vocal sung an octave lower.

BABYLON

Words and Music by STEFANI GERMANOTTA,
MATTHEW BURNS and MICHAEL TUCKER

Strut it out. Walk a mile. __ Serve it an - cient cit - y style. __

Talk it out. Bab - ble on. __ Bat - tle for your life, Ba - by - lon. __ That's

gos - sip. What you on? __ Mon - ey don't talk. Rip that song.

Gos - sip. Bab - ble on. __ Bat - tle for your life, Ba - by - lon. __

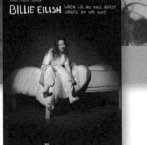